Serene Spa Success

Starting Your Own Profitable Day Spa

Table of Contents

Chapter 1. Introduction

Welcome to this Special Report: "Serene Spa Success: Starting Your Own Profitable Day Spa." Passion, relaxation, and financial freedom come together exceptionally in the spa industry. Are you ready to combine your love for wellness and your entrepreneurial spirit? Then this in-depth guide is designed for you! We take you by the hand through your journey, offering valuable insights and tools to help you establish a thriving day spa. You'll uncover essential tips, from selecting the perfect location to creating a soothing ambiance, hiring the right team, and beyond. By the end of this report, you'll be equipped to turn your vision into a profitable reality. Secure your chance to dive into a world of tranquillity that not only enriches lives but also promises attractive returns. Let's embark on the pathway to serene spa success together!

Chapter 2. Dream to Reality: Understanding Your Vision

Understanding your spa vision requires an in-depth awareness of many factors, from its core purpose and clientele to its aesthetic, services, location and profitability potential. This journey from dream to reality can seem daunting but, with clarity and careful planning, you can build a blueprint for success that aligns perfectly with your unique vision.

2.1. Define the Purpose of Your Spa

What is the main aim of your spa? Are you looking to provide a sanctuary of tranquillity for stressed-out city dwellers, or perhaps to specialize in specific treatments such as holistic therapies or advanced skincare? Your spa's purpose doesn't need to be singular; it can be multi-faceted. However, it must resonate strongly with you. After all, it's your passion for this vision that will motivate you every step of the journey and also resonate with your future clients.

When defining the purpose of your spa, consider your own interests and areas of expertise. If you're passionate about aromatherapy, for instance, a spa focusing on aromatherapy treatments could be a fitting choice.

2.2. Determine Your Target Clientele

Understanding who your clientele will be is integral to shaping your vision effectively. Consider age, gender, occupation, income, and lifestyles. Are you targeting busy professionals, health-conscious millennials, or luxury-seeking tourists?

Researching and reviewing demographic data could be insightful and aid in effectively determining your target audience. Once you have a clear picture of your potential clients, you'll be better equipped to design a spa experience that appeals directly to their needs and wants.

2.3. Establish Your Spa's Aesthetic

A central element of any spa is its aesthetic – the visual and stylistic components contributing to its overall sense of atmosphere and appeal. This involves everything from the architectural layout to the interior decorations, music, fragrance, lighting, and even the spa staff's attire.

Remember, your spa's aesthetic should align with both its purpose and its clientele. A spa intended to be a chic urban retreat, for instance, would likely have a minimalist, modern aesthetic. In contrast, a rural spa with a focus on natural health might favor rustic decor and materials, creating a sense of harmonious connection to the surrounding nature.

2.4. Decide the Range of Services You Will Offer

This is the tangible core of your spa experience: the services you offer. These could range from massages, facials, body treatments, hydrotherapy, nail services, and more – the choices are virtually endless.

It's essential, however, not to try to cover too much ground. Specializing in a few carefully-selected treatments can be far more effective, especially when starting out. These services should align with the interests of your target clientele, and match well with your own knowledge and experience.

2.5. Location, Location, Location

The importance of your spa's location cannot be overstated. The accessibility of your spa, the nature of the surrounding area and the type of building all significantly impact both your clientele and their experience.

Consider attributes such as parking facilities, proximity to public transport and local amenities, and of course, the cost of rent or purchase. Location is particularly important for footfall and visibility, so high street locations are often desirable, particularly for city spas.

2.6. Profitability and Sustainability: Your Financial Vision

The most beautiful vision and client-focused spa, in reality, cannot survive without addressing the essentials of profitability and business sustainability. Regularly forecast sales, costs, profits, and cash flow, adjusting as you learn more about your business. Always ensure you have the fund for emergencies, and the ability to invest in opportunities that could grow your business.

Remember, a profitable day spa is a sustainable one – a business that will carry on creating joy, promoting health and providing you with a rewarding livelihood long into the future.

By reflecting on each of these aspects in detail, you'll be crafting a strong, vibrant vision for your future spa – a picture of what your dream can look like once it's transformed into tangible reality. Your vision is the guiding light, illuminating the path forward on your spa journey. By understanding it thoroughly, you'll be better prepared to face the inevitably complex journey of turning your spa dream into reality with confidence, clarity and, above all, genuine excitement.

Chapter 3. Location Decisions: Sourcing Your Spa's Home

The first and foremost step towards opening your spa is finding the ideal location. This location would be the foundation of your success. As a spa owner, your goal is to have a location that is accessible, attractive, and suitable for the range of services you want to provide. Let's look at the many factors you need to consider to ensure you make the right decision.

3.1. Understanding Your Target Market

Before you start looking for a location, you need to have a clear understanding of your target market. What age group, gender, or income level are you targeting? Would your customers prefer a serene environment away from the hustles of the city, or would they rather have a conveniently located spa that they can visit during their lunch break or after work? Understanding your clientele will significantly impact where you establish your day spa.

3.1.1. Demographics

Conduct a demographic study of your preferred location. Look out for factors such as average income, lifestyle, and age. Your customer base largely depends on local demographics. For example, if your spa is located in a high-income neighborhood, you are likely to attract customers who can afford high-end treatments.

3.1.2. Socio-Economics

Understanding the socio-economic patterns of your prospective location is also crucial. Is the neighborhood predominantly residential or commercial? A locale with several businesses such as hotels or offices could provide you with clientele looking for services such as massage therapy to relax and unwind after a long day at work.

3.2. Sizing Up the Competition

It's essential to research your competition before setting up your spa. Are there any other spas nearby, and what type of services do they provide? If the competition is stiff, it might be challenging to penetrate the market — unless you can offer unique services that they don't. Patrons will always flock to the establishment that provides the best combination of price, service, and convenience.

3.3. Accessibility and Visibility

In addition to understanding your market and the competition, you need to ensure that your spa's visible and easy to access. It would be best to have ample parking space for your clients. The convenience of arriving and departing from your location is paramount. Accessibility by public transportation is another factor worth considering.

===The Building: Fit and Functionality

When choosing the building for your spa, consider if it's functionality aligns with your business plan. Evaluate the state of the architecture, plumbing, HVAC system, electrical fittings, and other necessary installations. You may need to modify certain parts to create privacy, an essential characteristic of a spa.

3.3.1. Leasing or Purchasing

The decision to either lease or purchase your spa premises depends on your financial capabilities. Leasing might be preferable for a startup due to its lower upfront costs. However, if you have the resources, purchasing the property offers more stability and freedom to customize the premises to your liking.

3.4. Evaluating Market Trends

Monitoring real estate market trends and economic indicators such as local business growth, increasing property values, and population growth can provide you with insights about the potential of the location. Locations with positive growth trends will offer you a larger customer base and better business prospects.

3.5. Seeking Professional Help

If deciding on a location becomes daunting, consider hiring a real estate agent. They have abundant knowledge about available spaces, pricing, lease agreements, and knowledge of the best neighborhoods to open your spa. They can guide you in choosing the perfect location within your budget.

3.6. Complying with Zoning Laws

Lastly, you must check with local authorities to clarify if your desired location complies with zoning regulations for businesses like a spa. Some residential areas may have restrictions on commercial activities. Non-compliance can lead to heavy fines, legal repercussions, and potentially, closure of your spa.

In conclusion, selection of location for your spa is where your dream business plan begins to become a reality. Much like a home, it needs thoughtful selection and fulfilling the criteria of your vision. The journey to finding the right location can be daunting but with the right mix of patience, diligence, market study, and professional help, it's achievable. Therefore, don't be afraid to take your time during this phase. Remember, a well-chosen location will lead you a step closer to your serene spa success!

Chapter 4. Creating Serenity: Design and Atmosphere in Your Spa

Your day spa's design and ambiance have a direct impact on your customer's experience. The interior should exude tranquility, promote relaxation, and reinforce your brand message. In this section, we'll delve into some key considerations, including aesthetic appeal, sound and scent management, and the composition of your service spaces.

4.1. Choosing a Design Concept

The first step in creating a soothing atmosphere for your spa is deciding on a design concept. This design should be coherent with your brand ethos and targeted client demographic. High-end day spas often lean towards modern minimalist or luxe classical styles, while holistic spas may incorporate elements of biophilic design, reflecting nature and organic forms.

You might want to hire an interior designer with spa design experience. They'll know how to create an environment that fosters relaxation and stress reduction. However, if you're working on a shoestring budget, there are plenty of online resources to draw inspiration from. Consider using an app like Pinterest to gather ideas and create moodboards.

4.2. The Role of Color

Color has an undeniable impact on mood and emotion. Therefore, it should be at the forefront of your design considerations. Commonly, spas use neutral and pastel colors, as they evoke feelings of calm and serenity. Blues and greens draw connections with nature and are proven to enhance feelings of tranquillity, while warm tones of beige, brown, or cream, can foster a cozy, serene ambiance.

Emphasize the use of color in different areas based on the mood you want to promote. In treatment rooms, cooler colors can facilitate relaxation, whereas in reception or retail areas, warmer tones might be more appropriate.

4.3. Lighting Matters

Strategic lighting is another integral part of creating a soothing ambiance. Softer, warm light tends to create a more relaxed and inviting atmosphere. Spotlights can be used to highlight certain areas or features, but their use should be sparing to avoid creating harsh shadows. A mix of natural and artificial lighting is ideal. Where possible, make the most of any natural light, as it's often considered the most flattering and can connect your space to the outside world.

4.4. The Importance of Acoustics

Sound management is often overlooked in spa design, yet it's crucial for creating a serene environment. The last thing a client wants when they are trying to relax is the interference of external noise. High-end spas invest in soundproofing to ensure that street noise or neighboring businesses do not disrupt the tranquility inside.

Consider also the sounds within your spa. Ambient sounds of nature such as running water, or gentle, relaxing music can be used to induce peace and relaxation.

4.5. Textures and Materials

The choice of materials and textures can greatly influence the ambiance. For example, the use of natural materials like wood and stone conveys an earthy, calming aura. On the other hand, marble and stainless steel can lend a more polished, high-end feel. Use texture to add depth and interest to your design; rich, luxurious fabrics can feel opulent and comforting, while smooth, cool materials might be refreshing and calming.

4.6. Furniture and Fixtures

Whilst style and aesthetic are important when choosing your furniture and fixtures, do not compromise on comfort. Consider ergonomic principles in your choices, particularly for treatment tables and chairs.

4.7. Scent Management

Our sense of smell can have a profound impact on our mood and emotional state. Aromatherapy utilizes this fact and is a common tool in relaxation and wellness. Carefully decide on the scents you want to permeate your spa. Lavender, for example, is well-known for its soothing qualities, while rosemary and mint can revitalize and invigorate.

4.8. The Final Touches

Attention to detail can make a significant difference in how your clients perceive their spa visit. The art on the walls, the quality of the linens, the selection of plants, and even the style of the service trays can all contribute to the overall ambiance.

Creating a serene and tranquil environment is key to the success of your spa. Patrons come to de-stress and escape from their hectic lives, and your spa's design and atmosphere play a huge role in aiding that escape. Design your space with thoughtfulness and careful attention to ensure that your clientele leave feeling refreshed and eager to return.

Remember, the design and ambiance of your spa should continually evolve to keep up with trends, continually surprise your regular clients and improve based on customer feedback. Your spa's atmosphere, after all, is an essential part of what sets you apart and keeps patrons coming back for more.

Chapter 5. Brick by Brick: The Basics of Building a Spa

When setting out to build a successful day spa, you must consider many different components. From your initial idea and planning stage to the construction and ultimate launch of your physical establishment, each step is integral to the overall success of your venture.

5.1. Getting Started: Concept and Vision

Your entrepreneurial journey begins with a concept and vision. Having clarity about what you want to achieve is fundamental for the design, orientation, and general execution of your project. Your concept will guide every decision made, from the spa's look and feel to the services it provides, roles of hires, branding, and operational practices.

Just as every other business, a spa needs a well-defined business plan. This document is not only necessary for securing financing, but it helps provide a roadmap for your spa's development and growth. A typical day spa business plan should cover essential elements such as market research, service descriptions, pricing strategies, marketing and advertising strategies, a detailed financial projection, and an operational plan.

5.2. Location, Location, Location

The location of your day spa can either strengthen or weaken your success. Hence, put considerable thought into selecting a suitable location for your spa. When reviewing potential locations, consider factors such as visibility, accessibility, parking, curb appeal, local competition, and demographic suitability.

Is it easy for clients to find and reach your spa? Does the surrounding environment align with the spa's ambiance you want to create? Are the neighbors similar businesses complementing or direct competitors potentially splitting your customer base? Observing these points helps ensure your spa aligns with your targeted client's needs and expectations.

5.3. Designing Your Spa

The design of your spa involves several considerations like layout planning, aesthetics, functionality, and safety codes. Work with a skilled architect experienced in designing spas and wellness establishments. They would understand the intricacies of properly laying out treatment rooms, locker rooms, relaxation areas, and retail spaces.

A well-designed spa should provide a soothing ambiance right from the entry. Colors, textures, lighting, and even scents should promote relaxation and induce a sense of well-being. Consider using sustainable and eco-friendly materials as this resonates with many spa-goers today.

Ensure your design complies with the standards set by authorities, in terms of hygiene, fire safety, accessibility, etc. You'll also need to plan for enough storage space for supplies and equipment, a designated area for laundry, as well as facilities like restrooms and changing rooms that cater to the comfort and convenience of your clients.

5.4. Building Your Spa

Once your plans are in place, your next big step is bringing your design to life during the construction phase. Adequate supervision is crucial to ensure that the project adheres to the pre-determined timeline and budget.

The right choice of a construction team is crucial. Just like an architect, it is beneficial to engage a construction firm experienced in spa construction. Such a firm could help balance your desires and budget by suggesting cost-effective materials and solutions without compromising on quality and aesthetics.

Throughout the construction, regular site visits should be conducted to monitor progress and detect any deviations from the plan early. It is not unusual for modifications to be required during construction, so try to remain flexible, open-minded, but clear about your non-negotiables.

5.5. Installing Equipment

For your spa to offer top-notch service, it's crucial to invest in high-quality equipment. Massaging tables, facial steamers, skin care machines, pedicure chairs, etc., should be comfortable, user-friendly, durable, and efficient. Analyze each piece of equipment considering how well it fits your menu of services, reliability, warranty, supplier's customer service, and certainly, the cost. Keep abreast of the latest innovations in spa equipment as technology continues to evolve.

5.6. Wrapping Up: Licenses and Certifications

Before you open the doors to your spa, ensure all legal requirements are met. Every region has its own regulations and requirements for businesses. Therefore, acquaint yourself with specific licensing requirements for spas in your area and ensure your spa meets all these standards.

Additionally, some clients may be attracted by certain certifications, like a "green" spa certification that signifies environmentally friendly practices, or a certification from a recognized professional body which signifies adherence to industry standards of service and professionalism. These types of certifications can add to your credibility and attract a specific clientele.

Armed with this insight, you're now ready to take the first step on your journey to opening a successful day spa. Remember, building a successful day spa is not an overnight process, but with the proper planning and execution, your spa can become a relaxing getaway for individuals seeking the ideal balance between wellness and pampering.

Chapter 6. Dive Into Finances: Budgeting and Funding Strategies

Before beginning your journey into the spa business, it is imperative to discuss the financial aspects. Proper budgeting and securing funding is key for your spa's success and profitability. So, let's dive deep into understanding the nitty-gritty of budgeting strategies and funding options.

6.1. Understanding Costs: Expenditure Breakdown

The primary step in planning your day spa's finances is to understand the types of costs involved. These can be broadly categorized into two: setup costs and operational costs.

Setup costs are the initial investments required to start the spa. They include:

- Lease/rent or purchase price of the location
- Spa equipment (massage tables, steam rooms, etc.)
- Renovation expenses
- Initial inventory of products
- Software and hardware
- Licenses and permits
- Initial marketing and promotional expenses
- Consultant or contractor fees

On the other hand, operational costs are recurring monthly or yearly expenses:

- Monthly rent or mortgage

- Salaries for employees

- Utilities (electricity, water, etc.)

- Maintenance costs

- Marketing expenses

- Insurance

- Inventory replenishment

Keep a detailed record of all these costs, as this will form the base of your budget. Understanding the number and types of expenses will help you make an accurate financial projection.

6.2. Projecting Revenue: How Much Will You Make?

The next step in your financial journey is revenue projection. Try to be realistic and avoid overestimating. Your revenue will primarily come from services and products:

- Spa services: These are the services you offer, like massage, facial, sauna, etc. To estimate your revenue, you need to forecast the number of services you expect to offer per day, week, or month. Then, multiply that by the price of each service.

- Retail products: If you stock wellness products for sale, this can serve as an additional revenue source.

Further, consider the seasons. Spa businesses often see more customers during certain times of the year, like winters or holidays. Make sure to factor this into your estimations.

6.3. Drafting a Budget

When the estimated expenditures and projected revenue are ready, the next task is to form a budget. A budget will give a clear picture of your business's financial health, assisting everyone from stakeholders to employees.

1. Begin by recording all expenditure and revenue numbers.

2. Deduct the total expenditure from your total projected revenue.

3. The remainder is your net profit or loss.

It is critical to reassess and amend your budget regularly, aligning it with realistic forecasts and business growth.

6.4. Funding Alternatives: Bootstrapping, Loans, and Investments

You might not have all the necessary funds to start your spa. In this case, you need to explore various funding options.

- Bootstrapping: This refers to starting the business using your own savings. The advantage of bootstrapping is that you're in full control, and there's no pressure to repay a loan or please investors. The downside is that the risk is entirely yours.

- Bank loans: Banks offer different types of loans for starting businesses. Before giving a loan, they will scrutinize your business plan and financial projections. So, it's crucial to have these at hand.

- Investors: Investors could be individuals or companies willing to finance your business in exchange for a share of the profits or equity in the business. While this is a great way to get funding, it does mean sharing your profits and possibly control of your business.

Remember, each type of funding comes with its own set of benefits and drawbacks. Thoroughly analyze each option before making a decision.

6.5. Potential Financial Challenges and Solutions

Being aware of potential fiscal challenges can help alleviate risks. Here are some common difficulties spa owners face and how to address them:

- Variable income: Since income can vary seasonally, it's important to have a financial buffer or savings for lean months.

- High initial investments: The initial investment can be hefty. Securing a loan or finding investors can help bear this cost.

- Unexpected expenses: Always count on surprise costs. Include a miscellaneous category in your budget for unforeseen expenditures.

In conclusion, careful planning and management of finances are key for a profitable spa business. Proper understanding of expenses, smart budget creation, astute revenue forecasting, and finding suitable funding methods will go a long way in making your spa venture a success.

Chapter 7. Pulling the Right Strings: Regulations and Licenses

To establish a successful spa, you need more than passion for wellness. It involves meticulous planning, a substantial investment of time, energy, and resources, and a thorough understanding of business operations. One of the most critical areas you need to understand is the regulatory landscape. This includes understanding the licenses you need to operate your business legally, and any restrictions on the services you can provide or the way you conduct your business. In this chapter, we delve into navigating these complex waters to ensure your venture is legal, safe, and prosperous.

7.1. Understand Local, State, and Federal Regulations

Before even purchasing a property, first familiarize yourself with the legal requirements of your city, state, and the federal government. You need to ensure that the spa services you plan to offer are legal and enshrined within the jurisdictions in which you operate. Depending on your location, different licensing departments will have different requirements and can vary remarkably.

Research carefully as these laws govern everything in your business – from the products you can use, the services you can provide, to the way you handle customer data. Moreover, penalties for non-compliance can be severe, including fines, penalties, and even the revocation of your license to operate.

National professional bodies like the International Spa Association (ISPA) may provide useful local and state-specific information, so do not limit your research to government resources only.

7.2. Obtaining a Business License

Operating any enterprise obliges you to have a standard business license. The process to get one varies, depending on your local government procedures. Typically, you'll need to check with your local city or county office, or the Small Business Administration (SBA) to discover specific requirements.

To obtain this license, you'll be required to complete an application form, provide proof of identity, demonstrate proof of property ownership or lease agreement, and pay a licensing fee. This fee varies depending on location and the size of the operation.

Remember, having a business license is not a one-time process. You need to ensure that your license is renewed regularly - many municipalities will require you to renew your business license annually or biennially.

7.3. Acquiring Health and Safety Certifications

Beyond the business license, spas often need to demonstrate compliance with health and safety regulations. This might require regular inspections and certifications that needs to be visibly posted in the spa. The exact certifications required will vary by state or even city, but all aim to ensure customer and staff safety.

You may have to take part in specific schemes or training to demonstrate your adherence to certain regulations. For instance, all staff must be trained to maintain hygiene standards in treatment rooms, ensure equipment is maintained correctly, and manage any client allergies or emergency situations that might arise.

Special attention should be given to cleanliness and sanitation requirements, as spas often come under scrutiny for these aspects. Regular cleaning schedules should be established and followed to ensure your spa remains within requirements.

7.4. Acquiring Professional License

Spa services often require professional licensing in specific areas, such as massage therapy, esthetics, cosmetology, and so on. These licenses require a particular level of training and education, usually determined by a state licensing board.

Each practitioner in your spa will require their own individual license to practice, and these licenses will often require regular re-certification or continuing education credits to stay valid. Being involved helps you to stay informed about any changes to these requirements, ensuring your staff continually meets the state requirements.

7.5. Alcohol Service License

If you plan to serve alcohol as part of your spa service, it's important to note that you'll need an additional license for this purpose. Alcohol service can be governed by both local and state laws. You should look into both your local and state requirements before deciding to offer alcohol.

7.6. Managing Legal and Regulatory Changes

Bear in mind that legal and regulatory requirements are not fixed. Laws and regulations can change, and it's your responsibility to keep up-to-date with recent developments. Subscribe to local, state, and federal business newsletters and regularly visit relevant websites to make sure you remain informed of any changes that could affect your spa business.

In conclusion, starting a successful day spa involves intricate understanding and diligent handling of numerous licenses and regulations. Considering the wide-ranging list of licenses and adherence to various regulations, it could feel overwhelming at first. However, by breaking the process down into manageable parts, keeping up with relevant changes, and obtaining necessary certifications, your venture into the spa business will be built on a robust legal and regulatory foundation, ensuring you and your clients the most serene experience. Lastly, consult with a business lawyer or a consultant who specializes in spa businesses for guidance through this complex landscape: it's an investment that will save you time and potentially costly legal mistakes.

Chapter 8. Soothing Services: Developing Your Spa Menu

An essential component of your spa's journey to prosperity is developing a comprehensive and attractive menu of services. Setting the stage for the client experience, your menu simultaneously represents your brand and serves as a critical marketing tool.

8.1. Identifying Your Niche

Imagine opening a restaurant without deciding what type of food to serve. The concept seems absurd. The same principle applies when you start a day spa. Before delving into specifics, it's vital to pinpoint your niche in the market. This niche should align seamlessly with your target audience, the scope of your services, and your overarching brand identity.

Consider industry trends, competitive landscape, and potential market gaps. Analyze what services are offered at nearby spas, and what they're missing. This knowledge can help you shape a unique and compelling brand. Remember, your spa doesn't have to be all things to all people. It's better to specialize and excel in specific areas.

8.2. Creating Your Menu of Services

Once you've identified your niche, it's time to turn those concepts into concrete services. Every service should inherently reflect your brand's character, whether it's focused on lavish luxury treatments, holistic wellness, or medically-driven procedures.

Ensure your services cater to a wide range of clients. Offer a combination of quick, affordable services (boosting client numbers and providing upselling opportunities) and high-value, luxury treatments (yielding higher profit margins).

Moreover, consider including innovative treatments that may not be found at other spas. This uniqueness not only intrigines potential customers but also secures a loyal clientele.

8.3. Pricing and Packages

Unsurprisingly, money matters significantly in the spa business. Set your prices too high and you risk alienating your customers. Too low, and you might struggle to turn a profit. Your pricing strategies should consider these key factors:

- Cost of operating your spa

- Market conditions and competition

- Perceived value of your services

Packages are another excellent way to boost business. Offering packages (a series of complementary services sold at a bundled, reduced rate) incentivizes customers to experience more services. Just make sure that your packages are reasonably profitable.

8.4. Seasonal and Special Offerings

Occasional menu shake-ups keep your spa fresh and exciting. Seasonal offerings can capitalize on changing weather conditions (like hydrating facials for winter or calming cucumber treatments for summer) while holiday packages or event-based promotions tap into clients' demands for festive pampering.

Additionally, consider partnership deals with local businesses. This not only opens up to new customers but exemplifies community spirit, further enhancing your brand image.

8.5. Retention and Loyalty Programs

Over time, retaining customers can be more cost-effective than constantly finding new ones. Loyalty programs can therefore be a game-changer.

Such programs might include offering every 5th treatment for free, or providing a discount for clients referring new customers. In the digital age, creating an app where customers can book services, track loyalty rewards, and receive exclusive offers can significantly enhance customer engagement.

8.6. Staff Training and Quality of Service

Last but not least, remember that a splendid service menu won't save your spa if the quality of services lacks. Your staff should be well-trained, professional, and dedicated to delivering top-notch services that leave customers feeling rejuvenated and appreciated. Regular in-house training sessions can further improve their skills and keep up with industry trends.

In conclusion, an outstanding spa menu isn't just a list of services. It's a reflection of your brand's unique identity. It's a strategic tool for customer attraction and retention. With the right amount of effort and insight, your spa menu can be a driving force behind your day spa's serene and successful journey.

Remember to always listen to your customers and adjust over time. What works today might not work tomorrow, and as a spa owner, your ability to pivot and adapt will play a considerable role in your long-term success.

Chapter 9. Team Harmony: Hiring and Training Your Staff

Your day spa is not a simple business. It's a sanctuary, a getaway, a place for people to escape daily stress and pamper themselves. The key to the success of such a wellness retreat is your team: a group of passionate, highly-skilled individuals who can promote relaxation, wellness, and peace. Hiring the right staff and ensuring they are properly trained is thus one of your crucial tasks.

9.1. Selecting Your Team

First and foremost, identify the kind of employees your spa needs. Typically, the day spa team includes massage therapists, estheticians, spa managers, and reception staff. Depending on your spa's services, you might also need nail technicians, hair stylists, and other specialists.

For therapists and other specialists, consider those who are not only licensed but who also have extensive experience. Here's a simple guideline:

1. Massage therapists - Look for those who are knowledgeable in various types of massages - Swedish, Deep Tissue, Hot Stone, Reflexology, and more. Ideally, they should have certifications to prove their competence in these areas.

2. Estheticians - They should be trained in performing facials, skin analyses, and body treatments. Knowledge in advanced esthetic treatments such as microdermabrasion and chemical peels is a plus.

3. Spa manager - A vital addition to your team. The spa manager

will handle the daily operations, marketing, and staff management. Therefore, choose someone with decent experience in managerial roles, preferably within the spa or wellness industry.

4. Reception staff - Choose employees who are friendly, organized, and have excellent customer service skills. They're usually the first-person customers encounter, making their role crucial to the overall client experience.

Always remember, however, that qualifications on paper only tell one side of the story. You must also look for passion and dedication in your prospective employees.

9.2. Training Your Staff

Once you've hired your team, it's important to invest in their training. It's not enough that they have the skills; they should also be aligned with your spa's vision and values.

Even if they come with a wealth of experience, don't skip essential and specific training. This can include several aspects like:

1. Service Training: Ensure your team knows how to perform each treatment or service your spa offers. Teach them the techniques, precautions, timings, and whatever else is necessary for a seamless and effective service delivery.

2. Product Knowledge: If you're selling products at your spa (like massage oils, skincare products, etc.), your staff should know these items inside out. This knowledge will allow them to confidently recommend and upsell products to customers.

3. Customer Service: No matter how skilled your personnel might be, if they can't interact effectively and politely with customers, it can sour the entire spa experience. Run regular customer service training sessions to keep their skills sharp.

4. Administration procedures: Particularly for your front desk staff and managers, they should be proficient in managing appointments, handling payments, and other administrative duties.

9.3. Staff Scheduling

Running a day spa often requires flexible scheduling. Depending on the demands of your clientele, the spa might need to be open early in the morning, late into the evening, weekends, and during holidays. It would be best if you had a clear scheduling system to ensure all shifts are covered, and your staff isn't overworked.

The key to successful scheduling is open communication. Be transparent with your staff about their work hours and make sure to consider their availability and preferences. Efficient staff scheduling can result in increased productivity and better staff morale.

9.4. Team Harmony

The success of your spa is not determined by individuals, but by how well your team works together. To foster a harmonious working environment:

1. Encourage open communication: Encourage your staff to voice out their thoughts, suggestions, and any issues they're facing. A listening ear can greatly foster good relations and collective growth.

2. Create a team-oriented culture: Organize team-building activities to strengthen bonds between your staff. A united team can better handle the stresses and challenges of the spa business.

3. Recognize and reward staff: Hard work should be acknowledged and rewarded. These can be simple gestures like verbal praise or more concrete rewards like 'employee of the month.'

Establishing a dedicated, harmonious, and effectively managed team is vital for your day spa's success. Be smart in your hiring process, ensure proper training, and foster a positive working environment. With such a team in place, you are well on your way to serene spa success.

Chapter 10. Satisfaction Guaranteed: Client Relations and Retention

Client satisfaction is the backbone of any thriving day spa business. It determines whether your clients will become loyal patrons and encourage others to visit your spa. Excelling in client relations and retention involves mastering direct client interactions, setting up excellent systems and procedures, creating an outstanding client experience, and continually evaluating your efforts.

10.1. Understanding Your Clients

Your first step in building a successful client retention strategy is understanding who your clients are. It's important to know:

- Their demographics: age, gender, income level, and occupation.

- Their needs, preferences, and pain points: What types of services do they like? What don't they like? What's missing for them at the current spas they visit?

Understanding these data points will allow you to tailor your operations, services, and marketing efforts to meet your clients' needs and exceed their expectations.

Use tools like client surveys, feedback forms, and CRM systems to collect and analyse this data. Remember to always ask for your clients' permission before collecting any personal information, and ensure you're compliant with all relevant data protection laws.

10.2. Creating an Outstanding Client Experience

Creating an outstanding client experience is key to client retention. Your clients' experience starts long before they walk through your doors and continues after they've left.

Your website, social media channels, booking process, environment and décor, staff interaction, service delivery, and post visit-follow ups all form part of your client experience.

A great client experience is consistent, personalized, exceeds expectations, and offers value. Consistency ensures your clients know what to expect every time they come to your spa. Personalization shows your clients that you see and appreciate them as individuals. Exceeding expectations makes your spa exceptional. Value shows your clients that they're getting their money's worth and encourages them to come back.

10.3. Training Your Team

Your team plays a significant role in the client experience you offer. Therefore, continually training your team is vital.

Ensure your team knows your brand values, services, products, and procedures. Teach them to provide exceptional service, from greeting clients warmly, offering personalized service, helping clients make suitable selections, to providing services professionally.

Regularly update your team's soft skills, product knowledge, and service delivery techniques. Consider motivation and incentive schemes to encourage high-performance and dedication to your vision of exceptional client experience.

10.4. Effective Communication Strategies

Effective communication is integral to building solid client relationships. It's important to communicate clearly and in a friendly, professional manner, whether it's in person, via phone, email, social media, or other channels.

Ensure your spa has policies in place about replying to client inquiries and complaints. These should detail response times, tones and language to use, and how to resolve various issues that may arise.

10.5. Setting up Loyalty Programs

Loyalty programs are a well-established technique to encourage repeat visits. Creating a program that rewards clients for their loyalty can give them a reason to come back. This could involve a points system, where clients earn points for every dollar spent that they can redeem for services or discounts.

10.6. Soliciting Client Feedback

Actively soliciting client feedback can be another effective way to build a strong relationship with your clients. They will appreciate the opportunity to share their thoughts and are likely to feel valued and heard, encouraging them to stay loyal to your spa.

There are many ways to gather client feedback, including comment cards, online surveys, social media, and feedback forms on your website.

10.7. Handling Complaints and Negative Feedback

No business likes to receive complaints, but they are an inevitable part of running a business. How you handle these complaints can make or break your client relationships.

Establish a clear process for handling complaints: listen to the client's concerns, apologize sincerely, rectify the issue swiftly, and follow up to ensure the client is satisfied with the resolution.

10.8. Regularly Review and Adapt Your Client Retention Strategy

It's important to regularly review your client retention strategy. This allows you to identify what's working well and what could be improved. Use client feedback and data from your CRM and point of sale systems to evaluate your performance.

Understanding client churn (i.e., losing clients) can help you address potential issues before they become significant problems.

A successful spa not only provides high-quality services but also prioritizes exceptional client relations. It listens to its clients and uses their feedback to continually improve its offering. The most competitive day spas are those that can retain their clients over the long term, ensuring a reliable revenue stream and a well-regarded brand. So, adopt these robust strategies to ensure genuine satisfaction, fostering long-term relationships with your clients. This will be key in turning your dream of running a successful, profitable day spa into reality.

Chapter 11. Spa Synonym to Profit: Marketing and Growth Strategies

Success in the day spa industry hinges on effective marketing and growth strategies—it's how you convert your passion and investment into profit. Let's explore the essential components involved in shaping and deploying strategic marketing plans that drive business growth.

11.1. Understanding Your Target Market

Before everything else, it's crucial to identify and understand your spa's target market. The demographic and psychographic profiles of your potential clients will inform your strategic approach to marketing.

Begin by defining your clientele's age group, gender, occupation, income level, and other relevant demographic factors. Next, consider their psychographic traits, including lifestyle attributes, buying habits, and wellness priorities. This dual approach will align your marketing efforts with your prospective customers' needs and interests.

11.2. Branding and Unique Selling Proposition

Your brand is the promise you make to your customers—it expresses your spa's identity and what sets it apart from competitors. It must reflect in your spa's name, logo, decor, and overall ambiance.

Your Unique Selling Proposition (USP) must be a key part of your identity. Articulate in a clear, compelling way what makes your spa special. This uniqueness could stem from your services (organic products used, exclusive treatments), your staff (expert therapists or personalized service), or your facilities (restful and serene ambiance, state-of-the-art equipment).

11.3. Establishing An Online Presence

In the digital age, maintaining an online presence isn't optional—it's a business imperative. A professionally designed website serves as an online storefront, enabling potential visitors to explore your range of services, pricing, and opening hours.

Social media platforms like Instagram, Facebook, and Twitter provide additional channels to reach your target audience. These platforms are excellent for showcasing your spa's atmosphere and treatments through high-quality images and videos. Stay active in your online interactions, listen to customer feedback, engage them in meaningful conversations, and address their concerns promptly. This engagement breeds loyalty and generates repeat business.

11.4. Search Engine Optimization

Search Engine Optimization (SEO) is a necessary tool to increase your site's visibility, making it easier for potential customers to find you. Carefully select keywords that are relevant to your business and include them in your site's content, meta descriptions, tags, and URLs.

Similarly, Google My Business (GMB) listing provides crucial visibility in local searches and maps. Here, you can showcase your spa's photos, services, and customer reviews. Strive to gather positive reviews to improve your rating and reputation.

11.5. Implementing Customer Retention Strategies

Acquiring a new customer is five times more expensive than retaining an existing one. Implement strategies that foster lasting customer relationships, such as a loyalty program that rewards repeat visits, or surprise perks like unexpected upgrades or free add-on services.

11.6. Collaborations and Partnerships

Local businesses and influencers can help you to reach more potential customers. For instance, you can collaborate with local hotels or fitness centers or work with influencers to create sponsored content or giveaways.

11.7. Seasonal Marketing

Plan marketing strategies to capitalize on holidays and other seasonal opportunities. Valentines Day, Mother's Day, and the Christmas season can offer themed treatments or gift vouchers as a timely revenue boost.

11.8. Measuring Success—Key Performance Indicators (KPIs)

Establishing KPIs helps you measure your marketing strategies' effectiveness. Key metrics can include client acquisition cost, client retention rate, and revenue per client. Regular review of these indicators will inform adaptive marketing strategies that sustain growth.

Remember, marketing is an ongoing process. It's important to consistently evaluate and adjust your strategy to meet evolving market conditions and consumer preferences. The infusion of creativity, data-driven insights, and customer-centric approach could be the catalyst propelling your spa into a profitable niche of success.

www.ingramcontent.com/pod-product-compliance
Lightning Source LLC
Chambersburg PA
CBHW071048260726
48661CB00007B/3206